BIG QUESTIONS

BIG QUESTIONS
BIG QUESTIONS

ABOUT GOD AND YOU

DAVID LAWRENCE

BIG QUESTIONS

'Unbelievably, Helena Christensen, the twenty-seven-year-old millionairess whose face gazes out from Dorothy Perkins shops across the country, whose body sells underwear exclusively for Playtex and Victoria's Secret, who has starred in several pop videos and once dated singer Michael Hutchence, is bored of her life. So bored, in fact, that she plans to quit modelling for good.'

WHAT! Run that past me again! Someone with everything that makes life worth living, bored?

It would appear to ordinary humanoids like you and me that Helena had life sorted. Done and dusted - and all by the time she was twenty-seven. After all, most of us believe that to be happy you need one or more of the following:

MONEY: **WE BELIEVE THAT ONLY WE COULD WIN THE LOTTERY, LIF WOULD BE GREAT.**

LOOKS: **WE BELIEVE THAT IF ONLY WE COULD BE THINNER/TALLER/SHORTER AND AFFORD REEBOKS/CALVIN KLEIN/KICKERS/LEVI'S (YOU DECIDE) WE'D BE MORE CONTENT.**

FREEDOM: **WE BELIEVE THAT IF ONLY OUR PARENTS WOULD GET OFF OUR BACKS AND LEAVE US FREE TO DO WHAT WE WANT, WE'D BE A WHOLE PILE HAPPIER!**

BE LIEVE ?

VE ?

RELATIONSHIPS:
WE BELIEVE THAT IF ONLY WE HAD A STEADY BOY/GIRL FRIEND (OR EVEN THE OCCASIONAL UNSTEADY ONE) WE'D FEEL MUCH MORE FULFILLED.

CAREER: WE BELIEVE THAT IF ONLY WE COULD GET A REGULAR JOB, LIFE WOULD BE ON THE UP STRAIGHT AWAY.

POPULARITY: WE BELIEVE THAT IF ONLY PEOPLE LIKED US MORE (OR MORE PEOPLE LIKED US) WE'D FEEL REALLY WANTED AND VALUED.

But what if there is something more to life than all the stuff which we believe makes us happy?

What if there is a spiritual dimension to life which needs to be dealt with?

Everyone's got a hunger, a hunger they can't resist. There's so much that you want, you deserve much more than this.
BRUCE SPRINGSTEEN

The more money you have, the more problems you have. I went from making no money to making comparatively a lot and all I've had is problems.
MADONNA

I refuse to believe that this is all and there's no more, otherwise there'd be no point.
MARK LANEGAN, SCREAMING TREES

How can I believe in God when just last week I get my tongue caught in the roller of an electric typewriter?
WOODY ALLEN

What if there
REALLY IS
A GOD ?

IS ANYONE THERE?

IS ANYONE

To believe that such a complex universe could be the freak bi-product of the Big Bang is just like believing that an explosion in Tesco's could accidentally produce a well-cooked four course meal! **Anon**

In the absence of any other proof, the thumb alone would convince me of God's existence!
Isaac Newton (scientist)

IS GOD THERE AT ALL? THAT IS THE **BIG** QUESTION.

And if God is there, and if he wants us to believe in him, why doesn't he give us some clues about where he is and what he is like? Well, here are four 'clues' that could point towards the existence of God:

We are all alone in a cold, lonely universe.
Richard Dawkins (scientist)

God has healed me completely and totally. It is wonderful when he mends a broken body but even more amazing when he mends a broken heart!
Jennifer Rees-Larcombe (miraculously healed by God from life-threatening encephalitis)

CLUE 1

THE WORLD, THE UNIVERSE (AND EVERYTHING)

The universe that we live in is incredible!

✱ Planets orbit without colliding
✱ The earth rotates at 24,000 miles an hour with split-second timing
✱ The environment is finely balanced so that each part depends upon the others to sustain life.

It's amazing! Could all this have happened just by accident? Does it not have the mark of some great designer?

THE INCREDIBLE WORLD ABOUT US IS A CLUE TO THE EXISTENCE OF GOD.

CLUE 2

PEOPLE!

All humans are absolutely awesome. The human brain is the world's most advanced computer. The way that humans can create and enjoy great music, blockbuster movies, chocolate cake (and loads of other stuff) sets us apart from the animal kingdom in a BIG way.

But why are we so different? The Bible gives us an answer when it claims that our uniqueness is down to being made to a different set of plans to the rest of life on earth. God made human beings to be like him - creative, intelligent, emotional and with the power to make choices.

THE SPECIALNESS OF YOUR HUMANITY IS ANOTHER CLUE TO GOD'S EXISTENCE.

CLUE 3

POWER

For many millions of people in the world today the most vital piece of evidence is the difference that God has made to their lives. Changes that people had not been able to bring about for themselves have happened when they have prayed and God has got on their case.

✱ People with life-threatening habits regain self-control.
✱ People with mind-crippling fears find peace.
✱ People plagued with guilt find forgiveness.

LIFE-CHANGING POWER AT WORK IN INDIVIDUAL LIVES IS ANOTHER CLUE TO THE EXISTENCE OF GOD.

IS ANYONE

IS ANYONE THERE?

THERE

No one

CLUE 4

No one SERIOUSLY doubts that nearly 2,000 years ago a man called Jesus lived in the country we now call Israel. The Bible contains four books about his life (by Matthew, Mark, Luke and John) and historical research has shown them to be reliable in what they tell us about Jesus.

On one level the Bible presents Jesus as a normal working-class human being. For example:
* He worked, ate, slept and talked * He got happy, sad, angry and frustrated *
He had a close family, good friends... and people who hated him!

But on another level Jesus was radically different.

1. HE ALLOWED HIS FRIENDS TO WORSHIP HIM (AWESOME)
2. HE HEALED SICK PEOPLE JUST BY TOUCHING THEM OR SPEAKING TO THEIR ILLNESS (EXTRAORDINARY)
3. HE COULD ALTER THE WEATHER JUST BY COMMANDING IT TO CHANGE (AMAZING)
4. THREE DAYS AFTER HE DIED AND WAS BURIED, HIS BEST FRIENDS - MUCH TO THEIR AMAZEMENT - MET HIM ALIVE AND WELL (STRANGE... BUT TRUE)

How are we to understand this **unique, world-changing life?** Jesus gave his own explanation when he told his friends that to know him *(Jesus)* was to know God.

Whoever has seen me has seen the Father. **Jesus**

Jesus claimed to be God himself, living as a human on earth! Amazing though it is, that claim does explain why Jesus on the one hand seemed so ordinary *(he was a man)*, yet on the other hand acted super-naturally *(he was God)*. Jesus wasn't just talk. He gave plenty of proof that he had the **sort of supernatural powers that we might expect of someone claiming to be God**. Jesus was GOD-IN-OUR-HANDS, GOD-COME-TO-EARTH, GOD-THAT-WE-CAN-SEE AND GOD-THAT-WE-CAN-UNDERSTAND. **The life of Jesus is the strongest possible clue to the existence of God - there's just no other way to understand him.**

JES

understand him

If God had a name what would it be...?

If God had a face what would he look like...?

What if God was one of us...?
Joan Osborne

The life of Jesus is the strongest possible clue to the existence of God - there's just no other way to understand him

Jesus: All the armies that ever marched, all the navies that ever sailed, all the parliaments that ever sat, all the kings that ever reigned, put together, have not affected the life of man on this planet as much as that one solitary life. Anon.

WHAT
IS
GOD
LIKE?

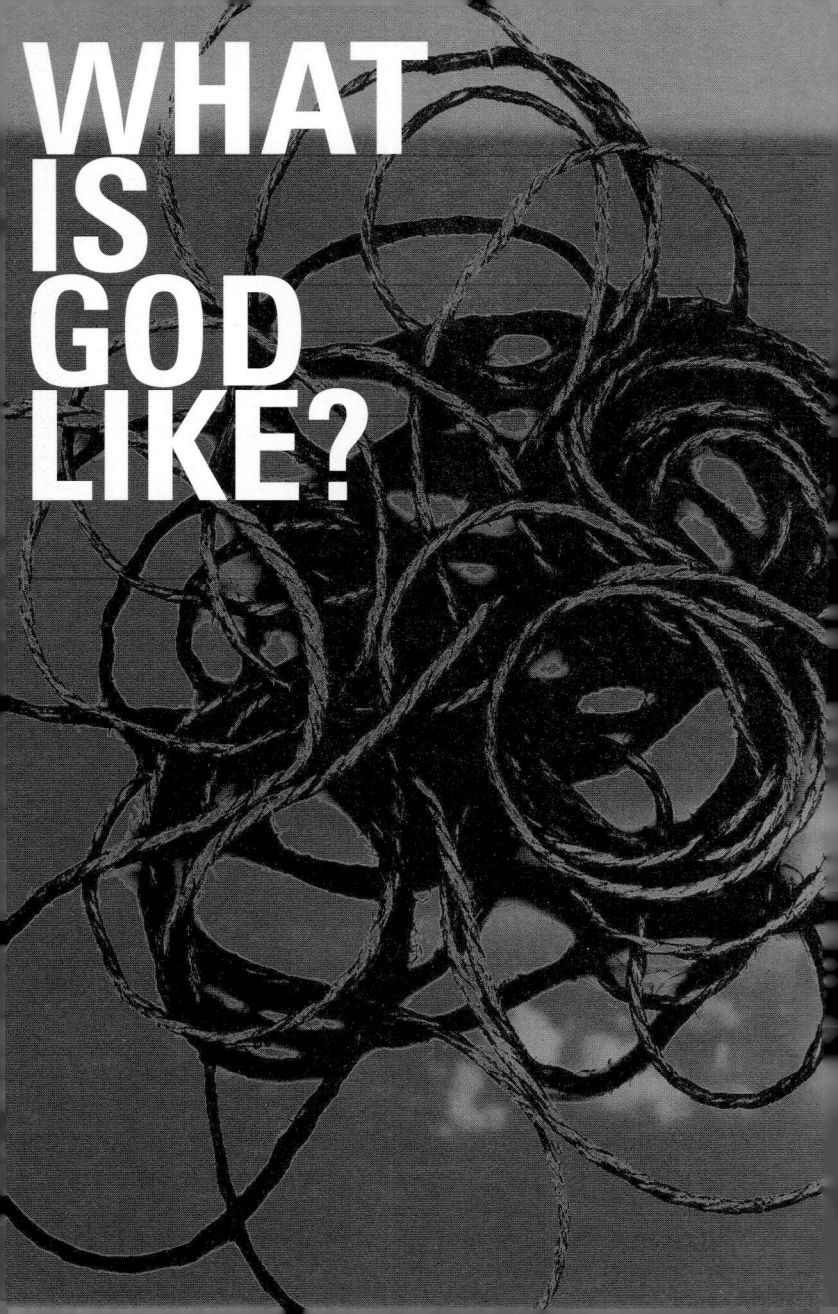

IF THESE CLUES DO POINT TO GOD, THEN WHAT IS HE LIKE?

But what is God like?

IS HE the God of our dreams (letting us do what we want and occasionally showing up to get us out of a tight spot) or the God of our nightmares (sneering at our best efforts and sending disasters to punish us when we put a toe out of line)?

HOW can we mere humans ever understand an invisible, universe-creating God?

THE ANSWER (as we began to see over the page) is that God has made it simple for us by living **on earth** in the shape of a human being, Jesus.

IN THE LIFE of Jesus, God was presenting himself on the stage of human history and effectively saying, 'Here I am. No more guessing games - this is what I am like!' By looking carefully at Jesus' life, we can understand the invisible God and know what he thinks about ordinary people - like us!

(There are all sorts of religions and beliefs in the world which come up with a picture of God. But if Jesus shows us what God is *really* like, then any picture of God which looks different to Jesus will have something missing. Beware imitations!)

> If only God would give me some clear sign! Like making a large deposit in my name at a Swiss bank.
> **Woody Allen**

> We look at this Son (Jesus) and see the God who cannot be seen.
> **The Bible**

SO what picture DID Jesus show us of the invisible God?

GOD IS INTERESTED IN FRIENDSHIP. Jesus took time to develop close friendships with ordinary people.

GOD IS INTERESTED IN LIFE. Jesus said that only with his help could people make sense of life.

GOD IS INTERESTED IN SUFFERING. Jesus helped loads of people with problems get their lives straightened out.

GOD HATES INJUSTICE. Jesus saw his life as being about confronting injustice, selfishness, and all forms of evil.

GOD RESPECTS HUMAN FREEDOM. Jesus never forced anyone to do anything. If people wanted to walk away and do their own thing, he let them go.

ALL THAT, AND NOT A THUNDER-BOLT IN SIGHT!

> No God,
> No life.
> Know God,
> Know life!
> **Anon**

> I have come to give you LIFE in all its fullness.
> **Jesus Christ.**

> Jesus is the exact likeness of God's own being.
> **The Bible**

WHAT DOES GOD THINK OF ME?

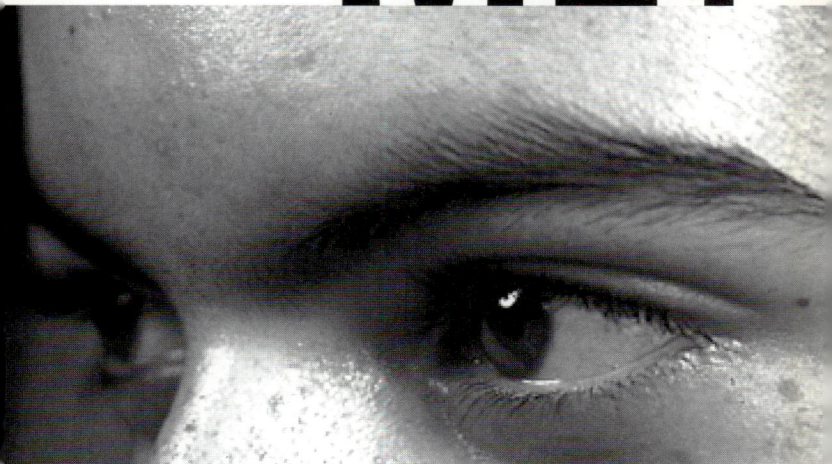

If you want to find out where Jesus would be hanging out, it'll always be with the lepers. **Bono.**

GOD THINKS YOU'RE GREAT!

JESUS SHOWED US THAT GOD <u>CARES ABOUT ORDINARY PEOPLE.</u> HE IDENTIFIED WITH US AND WITH WHO WE ARE. HIS CLOSEST FRIENDS WERE A REAL MIXTURE OF THE GOOD, THE BAD AND THE UGLY!

SO WE CAN BE SURE THAT GOD JUST LOVES TO DEVELOP FRIENDSHIPS WITH PEOPLE AND NO ONE IS TOO BAD, SAD OR HOPELESS FOR HIM - INCLUDING YOU.

GOD THINKS YOU'VE GOT A NEED.

JESUS SHOWED US THAT EVEN THE PEOPLE WHO THOUGHT THEY HAD EVERYTHING IN LIFE WERE STILL <u>INCOMPLETE</u> IF THEY SHUT GOD OUT. HAVING LOADS OF MONEY, BEING POPULAR OR HAVING A STEADY RELATIONSHIP ARE ALL OK BUT NONE OF THEM CAN BE A REAL SUBSTITUTE FOR A <u>FRIENDSHIP WITH THE MOST AWESOME BEING IN THE UNIVERSE!</u>

JESUS TAUGHT THAT REAL HUMAN HAPPINESS CAN ONLY BE FOUND IN A RELATIONSHIP WITH GOD - A RELATIONSHIP THAT HE OFFERS TO **YOU**!

GOD THINKS YOU'VE GOT A PROBLEM.

JESUS NEVER FORCED ANYONE INTO A FRIENDSHIP WITH HIM AND MANY PEOPLE JUST REFUSED TO HAVE ANYTHING TO DO WITH HIM. IN FACT IT WAS ALMOST AS THOUGH PEOPLE HAD A <u>BUILT-IN STUBBORN STREAK</u> WHICH MADE THEM PREFER TO CARRY ON <u>DOING THEIR OWN THING</u> RATHER THAN LISTEN TO WHAT JESUS HAD TO SAY.

IT'S STILL TRUE TODAY THAT ALTHOUGH GOD <u>THINKS WE ARE GREAT</u>, WE FREQUENTLY IGNORE HIM ALTOGETHER. THIS SELF-CENTRED, STUBBORN, GOD-AVOIDING INSTINCT IS WHAT THE BIBLE CALLS '<u>SIN</u>'. ITS PRESENCE IN OUR LIVES CREATES A REAL PROBLEM BECAUSE IT MEANS THAT WE LIVE IN GOD'S WORLD, <u>GUILTY</u> OF IGNORING HIM AND DOING OUR OWN THING.

JESUS SHOWED US THAT IF WE ARE TO ENJOY FRIENDSHIP WITH GOD, THIS SELF-CENTRED SIN-THING HAS TO GO - EVEN FROM YOU!

The story so far:

GOOD NEWS AND BAD NEWS!

The GOOD NEWS is that:
* God is there: we are not alone.
* He thinks we are great
* He wants our friendship.

The BAD NEWS is that:
* we have ignored him in our lives, so...
* we don't have a relationship with him and...
* we are guilty of living in a way that God does not approve of.

Many young people are suffering from the F-Factor; frustration, failure, fear and being fed-up!
Dr David Lewis
(youth psychologist)

God is good; we've just messed up.
Sinead O'Connor

Human beings have a lot of great inherent gifts but we're also very flawed.
Moby

I have come to give good news to the poor.
Jesus

HoPE?

hope?

So is there any

WHEN WE LOOK AT THE WORLD WE LIVE IN, IS THERE ANY HOPE?
AND DO OUR PAST MISTAKES MEAN THAT
GOD HAS GIVEN UP ON US? ARE WE JUST TOO BAD?
NO!
THE BIBLE MAKES IT CLEAR THAT
EVEN WHEN WE ARE AT OUR WORST,
GOD STILL HOPES FOR OUR FRIENDSHIP.
GOD IS INTERESTED IN US,
EVEN THOUGH WE'VE HAD NOTHING TO DO WITH HIM.
HE WANTS US BACK AND,
WHEN WE ARE READY,
HE CAN COMPLETELY OVERLOOK OUR PAST MISTAKES (SINS)
AND RELATE TO US NORMALLY.

WHEN AND HOW DID GOD DEAL WITH OUR SIN?
WHEN JESUS WAS EXECUTED ON THE CROSS 2,000 YEARS AGO.
THE BIBLE EXPLAINS THAT HIS EXECUTION WAS
NOT A PUNISHMENT FOR HIS CRIMES
(SINCE HE WAS DECLARED INNOCENT AT HIS TRIAL).

NO! ON THE CROSS JESUS:
* TOOK ALL THE PUNISHMENT THAT OUR GOD-REJECTION DESERVED
* MADE IT POSSIBLE FOR US TO BE FORGIVEN
FOR EVERYTHING WE'VE EVER DONE TO OFFEND GOD
* MADE IT POSSIBLE FOR US TO ENJOY
A NEW FRIENDSHIP WITH GOD,
JUST AS THOUGH WE'D NEVER BEEN APART!

AMAZING!

GOD DIDN'T KEEP HIMSELF TO HIMSELF; HE GOT INVOLVED.
STEVE CHALKE (TV PRESENTER)

GOD GOT US OUT OF THE MESS WE'RE IN AND RESTORED US TO WHERE HE ALWAYS WANTED US TO BE. AND HE DID IT BY MEANS OF JESUS CHRIST.
THE BIBLE

DO YOU BELIEVE IT?

THIS SOUNDS FAR-FETCHED (AND EVEN TOO GOOD TO BE TRUE) SO JUST IN CASE YOU THINK YOU'VE MISUNDERSTOOD, HERE'S THE DEAL AGAIN:

✱ GOD THINKS WE ARE GREAT! ✱ WE'VE IGNORED HIM AND RUINED THE GREATEST RELATIONSHIP WE COULD EVER HAVE ✱ HE IS WILLING TO FORGET THE PAST AND WAS EVEN READY TO DIE TO RESTORE OUR RELATIONSHIP WITH HIM.

THE BIBLE ACTUALLY PUTS IT THIS WAY:

'BUT HE (JESUS) TOOK OUR SUFFERING ON HIM AND FELT OUR PAIN FOR US. HE WAS WOUNDED FOR THE WRONG WE DID. HE CARRIED AWAY THE SINS OF MANY PEOPLE.'

CRUCIFIXION IS A TERRIBLE WAY TO DIE AND THE FACT THAT JESUS WENT THROUGH WITH IT IS PROOF OF HIS LOVE FOR YOU (AFTER ALL, DOES ANYONE ELSE LOVE YOU ENOUGH TO PAY WITH HIS LIFE FOR YOUR MISTAKES?).

WE CAN'T WORK OUR WAY BACK INTO A RIGHT RELATIONSHIP WITH GOD. GOING TO CHURCH, READING THE BIBLE OR GIVING AWAY OUR LAST ROLO WILL NEVER HEAL THE RIFT IN OUR RELATIONSHIP WITH GOD. OUR ONLY HOPE IS TO TRUST THAT THE GREAT SACRIFICE THAT JESUS MADE FOR US ON THE CROSS WILL DO THE JOB FOR US.

Jesus said, there is the house but I am the gate, kind of thing. Tony Mortimer **(East 17)**

Our hope lies not in the man we put on the moon but in the man we put on the cross. Don **Basham**

WHAT IS ON OFFER?

OFFER

Being willing to change our priorities simply makes space for God to get in on our act and start to work. As you start to relate together, God wants you to experience some FREE GIFTS:

✱ a new friend: the gift of never being alone. God has promised to stick with you through all of life's ups - and downs

✱ a clean start: the gift of knowing that every mistake and failure has been completely and utterly forgiven

✱ a new power: the gift of experiencing God's power at work in you. He is with you, enabling you to overcome difficulties that previously defeated you

✱ a new family: the gift of belonging to God's family - the church. (All believers everywhere - that's what the church is. They will be pleased to encourage you as you build your new friendship with God.)

✱ a new future: the gift of a relationship with God that lasts for ever. God promises that this life isn't the end - even when your body dies, God has a future planned for you!

781856 690928

When someone becomes a Christian (s)he becomes a brand new person inside... A new life has begun!
The Bible

Knowing Jesus means that I don't need to pretend - no more trying to prove something. God broke through the mask I hid behind; he freed me.
Martyn Smith (student)

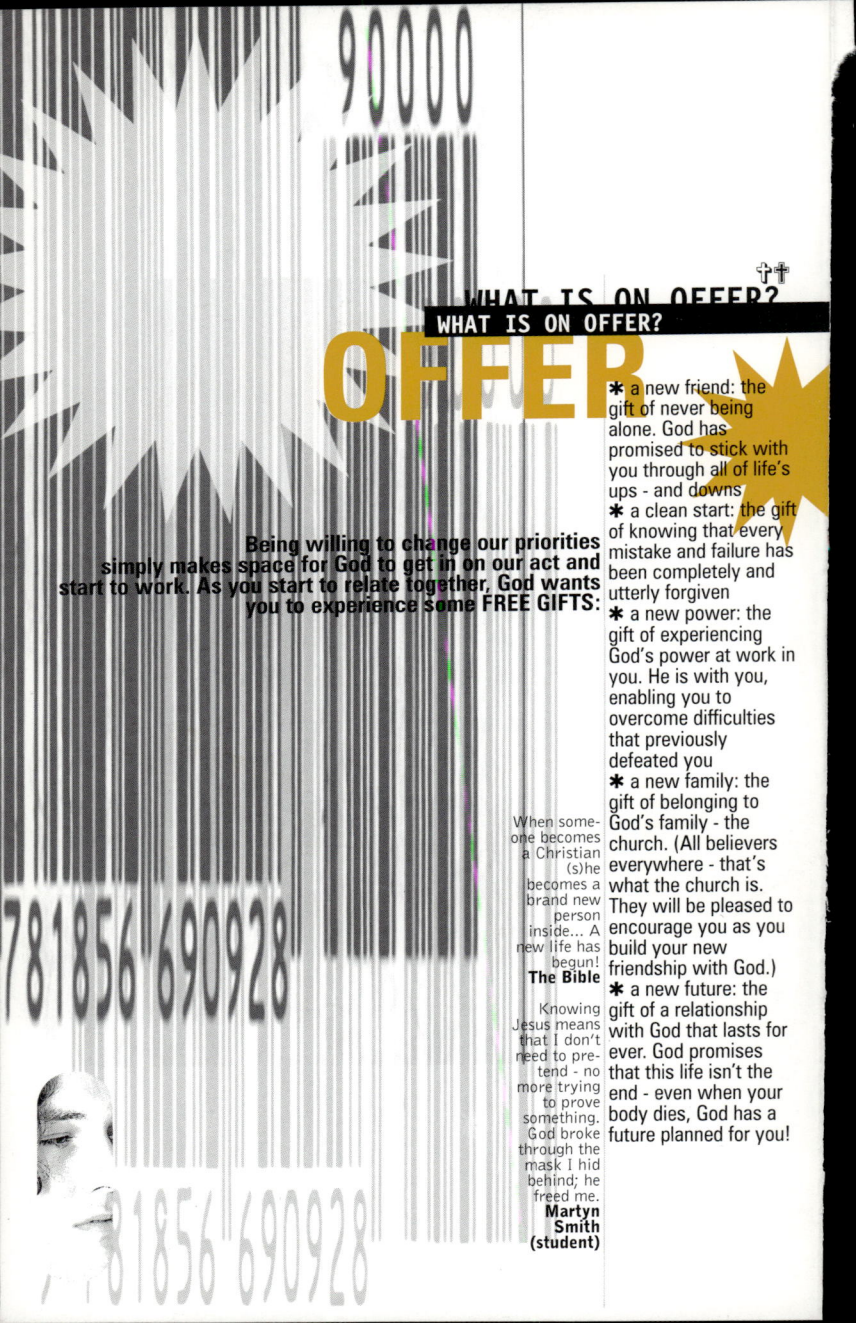

WHAT HAVE I GOT TO LOSE?

WHAT HAVE I GOT TO LOSE?

So is that it? Just believing that Jesus paid my dues allows me to enter into a new relationship with God? Well, there is one other thing - you've got to be ready and willing to make a few c   h   a   n   g   e   s   .

You see, before God can start to make a difference to your life, the things that used to pull your strings have to be put in his hands t   o   o   .

Normally, we allow different pressures to shape our lives: things like fashion, the media, the music industry and the pressure of   our   friends'   opinions.

It's not that any of these things is necessarily wrong but simply that none of them should rule our lives, when God's way is best. (After all, he created us.)

If God **does** exist and if he **is** the ultimate being in the whole universe then it makes a whole lot of sense to let **him** call the shots in our lives.

So what have you got to lose? How about   giving   it   a   go?

Those who give up their lives for me will have   new   lives. **Jesus**

I won't change - not unless the geezer with the big beard lands down in front of me and pulls a giraffe out of his nostril and goes, 'I'm God'. **Liam G   a   l   l   a   g   h   e   r**

My faith is fundamental to me and directs all other areas of my life. **Jonathan   Edwards**

who is in control?

WHAT DO I DO?

WHAT DO I DO?

If you are sure that God exists and wants a friendship with you, can you really afford to go on ignoring him? Maybe you have decided that it's time you got your act together with God by starting life anew with him at the wheel rather than in the back seat! *If so, here are four steps for you to take:*

THINK!

Think about what it's going to cost you to put God first in your life. What if your mates think you're mad or your parents think you've gone potty? Are you ready to risk it?

TURN!

Make a decision to *turn* your life over to God. Remember it's all or nothing. He is the first person you should turn to, no matter what. God doesn't want to be just one more brick in your life's wall! He is GOD and deserves to be accepted as number one - what he thinks counts!

TRUST!

Trust that Jesus has done everything necessary to make you be completely accepted to God. Don't worry that you've been too bad in the past or that you might not be good enough in the future. Remember that Jesus has paid for every shortcoming in your life - past, present and future!

TELL!

Tell God that you now mean business with him. How? You could use the words on the next page and make them your own.

Still not sure? Turn to last page.